PUEBLO AND NAVAJO
INDIAN LIFE
TODAY

Kris Hotvedt

With Illustrations by the Author

SUNSTONE
PRESS

Santa Fe
New Mexico

First Edition

Printed in the United States of America

10	9	8	7	6	5	4	3	2	1

Library of Congress Cataloging in Publishing Data:

Hotvedt, Kris, 1943-
    Pueblo and Navajo Indian life today / Kris Hotvedt; with illustrations by the author..
        p. cm.
    ISBN 0-86534-204-0; $8.95
    1. Pueblo Indians—Rites and ceremonies. 2. Pueblo Indians—Social life and customs. 3. Navajo Indians—Rites and ceremonies. 4. Navajo Indians—Social life and customs. I. Title
E99.P9H67   1993
973'.04972—dc20   93-14236
                              CIP

Published by SUNSTONE PRESS
Post Office Box 2321
Santa Fe, NM 87504-2321 / USA

CONTENTS

PREFACE

When I first saw Kris Hotvedt's woodblock prints several years ago, they appeared to be childishly simplistic or outright "primitive" depictions of Pueblo and Navajo life. Perhaps this accounts for their distinctive charm and continuing appeal. They reflect the emotional impact of their scenes without too much concern for perspective and facial detail. But guiding the cutting of these woodblocks is the hand of an artist who knows what she's doing, and the heart of a woman with a devoted love for Southwest Indian gatherings in all weathers.

She begins this small book with Kings' Day, January 6, and follows the calendar with the spring ditch cleaning, the summer Pueblo Corn Dances, to All Souls Day, the animal dances, powwows, throw-aways, and the Navajo Fair in late September. Composite scenes of people watching ceremonial dances, eating fry bread and mutton stew, appraising sheep—people shown inside and outside of pueblo rooms at the same time, with a big, round, red sun or moon overhead. How suggestive they are! They remind us local Southwesterners of the ceremonial dances and social fiestas we have attended, and they show at a glance the warmth and fun a new visitor will experience.

The text accompanying each illustration is just as simple. Informative to children as well as grownups, it briefly tells the ages-long traditions behind these current events without going into technical explanations.

One need not attempt to explain the growing popularity of these woodblock prints, now available in book form. The mystery of their appeal lies in their warm homeyness which evokes the beat of a drum, the smells of roasting chiles and tortillas, firelight and moonlight on a snowy winter night. And most of all perhaps, they remind us of a communal life our modern society has lost, the joy of gathering together without the need for commercial amusement.

Frank Waters

INTRODUCTION

Each year in the Southwest thousands of visitors from all over the world attend the various ceremonial dances of the Pueblo people, the Navajo Nation events, and Southwestern powwows. Many visitors arrive with a knowledge and understanding of these events. For other people these are totally new experiences, and a door is opened to unfamiliar ways of life, customs, traditions, and beliefs that have existed for hundreds and sometimes thousands of years, long before this country was called America.

These woodcuts and drawings depict some aspects of Pueblo and Navajo Indian contemporary life: the small things that compose the communal aspects of life and provide a sense of continuity in their relationship to traditional and ritualistic events.

The images are about communal ditch cleanings, about women working together on feast days, about waiting for the beat of the drum that sounds as if it is coming from the center of the earth, about Rivermen and koshares, and about people gathering together on certain days each year.

They are about the Navajo Nation fairs: powwows, food booths, fry bread contests, and parades. They are about women in velvet blouses and full skirts and men in Western clothes and hats, and about many people coming together for a few days for a special and good time.

This collection represents a small segment of the lives of the Navajo and Pueblo peoples, two diverse groups who are an important part of the life of America today.

After the first edition of *Fry Breads, Feast Days, and Sheeps* was published, people asked which came first—the woodcuts or the text? The visual images came first. They were done over a period of several years and were not intended as book pieces. However, people often asked for the stories behind the images.

After I corresponded with Frank Waters, he suggested I write about the events in my woodcuts and said the two presentations would go well in a book. At about the same time, a gallery director in Arizona, after looking at the woodcuts, commented that the pieces were documentary and should be used for a book.

Because the visual images came first and the text second, and since this is a book of woodcuts and the purpose of the text is not technical detail but explanation of visual image and introduction to Navajo and Pueblo life, the text was written in a simple style so it could be read by families and used in school programs. There are books available that go into great technical detail, and that is not the purpose of this publication.

Before the first edition was published, people from several pueblos read each page for content, intent, and accuracy. For this second edition, I was asked by Pueblo people to add a few pages concerning behavior, manners, and dress at Pueblo events, and I have done so. Please keep in mind that customs vary at each pueblo, and most of these images concern southern pueblos.

The visual images are woodcuts, linocuts, and combinations of wood and linoleum. The original woodcuts and linocuts are for the most part in two, three or four colors; there are bright orange or gold moons, red suns, earth-tone backgrounds, blue water cascading in the throw day images. If the print is one color, it is a dark purple. The originals are hand printed with a spoon on rice paper

HINTS FOR VISITORS TO PUEBLOS

About Questions—Don't Ask Them

A Pueblo woman said to me, "Well, I hope you say in that book that visitors to pueblos should not ask questions. They should just watch and enjoy, but they shouldn't ask any questions about anything."

In some cultures asking questions is a sign of politeness and a way of expressing interest; the reverse is true concerning Indian religion, dances, ceremonies. It is impolite to ask questions, and it is considered equivalent to being "downright nosey."

Because the dances are religious and their purpose is not that of entertainment, even when there is obvious humor involved, and because the religion is by its very nature secretive and mysterious, questions should not be asked, even seemingly very innocent questions: about the role of a particular dancer, the meaning of a dance or gesture, or the parts of costumes.

Do not even ask the children questions about the dances, their roles in the dances, or their costumes. The children, no matter how young, already know that religion is private and not to be discussed with outsiders.

Because the religious ceremonies are highly complex, tightly structured, and metaphysical, there is no way to give a simple meaningful answer.

In Judeo-Christian religious ceremonies, humor is usually separate from the "seriousness" of a religious service. There are no clowns, bawdy or silly gestures, or humor because it is a "solemn" event. In many Pueblo ceremonies, the dual sides of man and nature are confronted at the same time. There is not a separation of religion and everyday life; there is the religious in all life. The complexities of human nature are recognized, accepted, and confronted. During a winter animal dance, for instance, there might be "clowns" wandering around the plaza, and the men singers might be wearing humorous costumes. A first-time visitor might wrongly think the ceremony is entertainment and that it is OK to talk a lot, ask questions, and generally behave as if one is there to be entertained.

It is not OK.

Sometimes on the day of a summer corn dance, there will be a carnival at the edge of a pueblo, which will include carnival rides, amusement, and food booths. There also might be an area where pottery, rugs, jewelry, and other handmade items are being sold. This does not mean that the corn (tablita) dance is for entertainment; it isn't. And most likely, the people involved in the dance, in feeding guests, and in watching the dances have only a peripheral awareness of the carnival. A person attending the carnival and the ceremony should adjust tone of voice and manners for each place.

Remember, the ceremonies, even in the midst of humor, are not being held for amusement or entertainment. It is not OK to ask questions. Also, do not clap at the end of a dance. It is best just to watch and enjoy quietly.

Meals, Manners, and Dress

The Pueblo people go through many days of preparation for any event: religious preparation, food preparation, cleansing of the village itself, and private religious practices.

The women spend days preparing food for their families and guests. Visitors who are invited to eat at a Pueblo house should remember that this is not a party; the visitor does not have to entertain the other guests, talk loudly, ask questions, or make introductions. If there are Indian guests present, the non-Indian guests can follow their lead.

People will be coming to the house all day, so guests should not stay at the table too long or engage in too much conversation. Eat and then leave the table to make room for others, and be sure to thank the women who are serving the food. Then if there is room, it is OK to sit in another room. Sometimes it is very pleasant to sit in the house for a while, to sit with other people in relative quietness; quiet conversation is acceptable.

Visitors should not climb up on roofs or walls, unless invited to do so, and should be careful where they stand and sit, so they don't block anyone's view or get in the way of the dancers. At some pueblos, visitors are not allowed to stand in certain areas; in that case, a pueblo official will tell the visitor to move to a different location.

Never try to enter a kiva or any building the dancers are seen entering or leaving, and do not climb the kiva steps.

In the pueblos south of Santa Fe, cameras and recording equipment ARE NOT allowed; visitors should not carry a camera, even if it is in a case and picture taking is not intended. In pueblos north of Santa Fe, photographs might be allowed on certain days, and there is usually a fee for a camera permit; ask permission at the Governor's office. Sketching is not allowed at any pueblo.

Visitors going to a Pueblo or Navajo event should dress comfortably but appropriately. If it is a winter dance, be prepared for cold and wind with warm jackets, gloves, hats, and boots. In the summer, remember, this is not beach country; short shorts, halter tops on women and no shirts on men are not acceptable modes of dress. Dress comfortably but respectfully.

It is advisable in any weather to have a hat and clothes that can be layered. In the Southwest, the temperature can drop considerably by late afternoon or evening.

This may sound like a lot of "don'ts," but simply remember to attend any event with respect, manners, and common sense.

Guests at any event should realize that none of the events of the day are being done for the visitors. There is a form to the day. Let the day unfold around you, and watch and enjoy—quietly.

KINGS' DAY
(RIO GRANDE PUEBLOS)

It is Governors' Day, Kings' Day, January 6th, the day all the pueblos have new Governors and officers.

Because the man of the house has been given an honored position in the traditional life of the village, it is a busy day in this household. The women, while dressing in the traditional black mantas and preparing for the dances that will be held in the plaza in the afternoon, are giving instructions to other women helping in the kitchen.

The Governor and his aides come to the house and tell the people to dance. Many people come to the house to offer their congratulations and are invited to have something to eat; and all day the house is filled with quiet conversations in the tribal language and English.

Several men load a car with boxes and bags filled with oranges, packages of cookies, soda pop and many things for the "throw" that will be held later in the day. (After the dances are over, the Governor, his aides, and the dancers will "throw" from the roof tops to the people standing in the plaza.) Finally the car is filled with the boxes and the car, with its trunk open and doors barely able to close, is slowly driven to the other side of the plaza.

Inside the house the aromas of chile, oven bread, stews, and coffee fill the air. There is a lot of activity in the house with people leaving to go to the plaza to watch the dances, returning to eat and get warm, children playing, and women visiting and working in the kitchen.

In the evening, after the dances and the "throw," the house will be filled with friends and relatives coming to pay their respects to the man and his family.

Kings' Day

PUEBLO IN THE SNOW
(San Felipe Pueblo)

As the winter afternoon turns into evening, the family gathers in the kitchen, which is filled with the aroma of chile stew and freshly made fry bread. Someone brings in an arm load of wood for the wood-burning cook stove; someone else puts the big bowls of beans and chile on the table, and everyone gathers around the long table.

After eating, everyone is content and warm, and events of the day and stories of long ago are told.

A middle-aged family member tells the young people how life was before electricity and television came to the pueblo, how life was before everyone had cars and trucks, as well as jobs in nearby cities.

She tells of long, quiet winter evenings when everyone sat on the floor around a big bowl of popcorn, with only the light and warmth from the corner fireplace, to listen to her grandfather telling stories.

She tells how he would sit on the floor with his moccasined feet crossed, his hair in the traditional "chonga," and his lined face expressive of the emotions of the stories; and of how he would tell stories of the old days, stories that were funny, stories that were frightening, and stories that carried the history of the Pueblo people to the next generation.

She is afraid that these stories will be lost, that the stories won't get passed down to the younger generation now that everyone is so busy watching television and traveling around by car.

But the stories won't be lost, for they are being told once again on this winter night.

Pueblo in the snow

WINTER DANCE
(Cochiti Pueblo)

It is late morning on a cold but sunny winter day and a few people, wrapped in colorful striped blankets, are waiting patiently in the plaza for the dances to begin.

The old adobe house on the corner of the plaza is filled with family and friends. The house has been added to many times over the years; some of its rooms are among the oldest in the village, and its rooms hold large gatherings of people.

In the kitchen it is warm, food is being served, and people are eating and talking quietly at the long table.

Other people are sitting in the front room talking and watching television, and the children are playing with two small goats they have brought into the house.

At last, the sounds of the drums can be heard and the singers enter the plaza. Upon hearing the drums, some of the people in the house go to the porch, and others, climb the steep outside stairway to the roof to watch the dances.

Winter dance

THE DANCES ARE ALMOST OVER
(Cochiti Pueblo)

It is a day of the winter animal dances, and the male singers in the plaza are dressed like various ethnic and religious groups and other Indian tribes. They are dressed with great exaggeration and, for amusement, they are often dressed as the opposite sex.

In the center of the plaza are the "animals" — buffalo, deer and antelope. The deer and antelope figures lean forward, their arms outstretched and downward, resting on short sticks, and in their costumes and with their antlers they appear as the actual animals. The buffalo in their headdresses and dance kilts, and the buffalo women, dance up and down the rows of animals. The buffaloes, who have healing powers and bring snow, look larger than life as they lead the lines of animals across the plaza.

The spectators watch with great respect, stand back and give the animals a lot of room, for these dances are like tapestries rich in symbolism. They are acknowledgement of the cycles of life, and the integration of the lives of all living creatures on the earth; they are full of thanksgiving for what the earth provides, a pageantry of the hunter asking for the animal to come to him, to provide for him. They are blessings and prayers for the animal and the life of the animal as it lives on in man. These dances are powerful ceremonies of life's forces.

The children watch the dances quietly and with awe. Sometimes late in the day, the children will pretend that they too are deer and antelope as they lean forward on short sticks, look about them, and dart to new positions and formations. Sometimes they hold clumps of tumbleweed on their heads and pretend that they too have antlers as they dance around each other.

These children experience rare childhoods steeps in the expressive forms of the cause-and-effect of life's forces and cycles, and the integration of the religious in all aspects of life.

The dances are almost over

LISTENING TO THE QUIET
WHEN THE DANCES HAVE ENDED
(San Felipe Pueblo)

The animal dances are exquisite and powerful dramas; because of the profound nature of the dances, the people sit silently for a few moments after the "animals" and singers have left the plaza.

It is very quiet now, and a mother dog and her pups create the only activity as they saunter across the plaza.

Pulling shawls and blankets and jackets around them, people slowly begin to leave; they speak in quiet voices as they walk home.

The drumbeat has ended and its absence has created a noticeable silence.

Listening to the quiet when the dances have ended

SPRING DITCH CLEANING
(San Felipe Pueblo)

Each spring, just about the time that winter seems to refuse to leave and spring seems hesitant to arrive, the irrigation ditches are cleaned of the year's debris.

The men of the village clean many miles of ditch, an important annual event for several reasons. The ditch brings water to the fields, and the fields provide food for the people. It is also an important time for the men as they work together on their land; prayers are said, storytelling takes place, laughter and meals are shared.

It is a communal work event that bonds together men of all ages and provides a service for the pueblo.

Spring ditch cleaning

LUNCH BREAK: CORN DANCE
(SAN FELIPE PUEBLO)

It is May 1st, the day of the Corn Dance. By noon the senses start to feel overwhelmed with the sounds of the drum, rattles, and singing, the colors of the spectators and dancers' clothing, the colors of the banner framed against the sky, the movement of the fir branches that each dancer holds, and the movement of the dancers.

Then suddenly it is time for the lunch break.

In the kitchen there is a wood stove and a long table. The spoons and forks are standing upright in a water glass in the center of the table, and there is a bowl and cup at each place setting. On the table are bowls of red and green chile, posole, stews, oven bread, and fry bread.

People eat quietly and there is very little talking. When people finish eating, they thank the women for the food and then leave the table so that other people can sit down.

The family members who have been dancing come into the house but do not eat heavily because they will be dancing for many more hours.

People sit in the other room and talk quietly; many times people do not talk at all; they are comfortable being together in silence.

Soon the lunch break is over, and everyone says "thank you" again and returns to the plaza to watch the continuation of the dances.

Lunch break: Corn Dance

THE COMING OF THE RIVERMEN
(Cochiti Pueblo)

For the children in the pueblo, this has been a long-awaited day. For weeks in advance they have asked each other, "Did the Rivermen go to your house last year? What happened? Will they carry me away to the river?"

Early in the morning, on Mary 3rd, the Rivermen "come from the river" and go to the church. They then start on their walk around the pueblo with whips in hand, bags over their shoulders, yelling "Whooooo" in high, scary-sounding voices.

There are usually eight Rivermen, and they walk through the village in two groups of four men. When the children see the Rivermen coming, they yell in Keresan and English, "Here they come! Hide! They're coming!"

The Rivermen stop at various houses and if the children have behaved well all year, the Rivermen bless the house, and the children put soda pop, cookies, and candy in the Rivermen's bags. If a child isn't going to participate in the Corn Dance in the afternoon, the Rivermen tell the child to dance for them. If a child has been behaving badly, two Rivermen will take the child and start to carry him to the river. (This is prearranged with the parents.) It gets very exciting at this point and everyone watches with great anticipation. Then the child's mother, or another relative, will run after them and "rescue" the child from the Rivermen.

Around noon the children put on their dance clothes and go to the practice houses. In the afternoon the children participate in a Corn Dance. The Rivermen are in the plaza also, and they crack their whips on the ground and in the air and dance around in the plaza with the children.

The Rivermen walk like young slim men, although with their heavy coats and what looks to be a bit of padding, they appear to be older men. They are in good disguise, and the children will never know if the Rivermen are older brothers, uncles, or fathers, or if they indeed "come from the river."

The coming of the Rivermen

GRAB DAY
(Cochiti Pueblo)

In the morning the foot races take place in the plaza: the men's races, the women's races, and the children's races.

Then it is time for the throw. Many people are gathered about a house and at first the crowd is quiet. Then there is excited cheering and yelling, and the people on the roof throw as fast as they can, and a hundred things seem to be flying off the roof at once.

Here comes a box of crackers, and someone over there just got hit with a can of soda, and there a melon landed on the ground and splattered all over everyone, and here comes a bucket of water. And rolls of toilet paper and paper towels come streaming down over the crowd.

It is fun and fast and then it is over, and people saunter on to the next house that is "throwing". By this time some people have filled laundry bags with their catch, and some of the women have doubled up their aprons to hold their goods, and most of the children are getting quite filled up with candy and soda pop, and everyone is having a good time.

Grab day

ON THE ROOF THROWING
(Cochiti Pueblo)

The family members take boxes of the throw goods to the roof. There are many boxes heaped with crackers, cookies, candy, soda pop, melons, balloons, beach balls, canned food, and many other items. What is being thrown today is quite different from what was thrown a century ago.

And as it is a summer throw, buckets and hoses are also carried to the roof, and the buckets are filled with water.

Soon the village people gather around the house and the throwing begins. The very young children in the family cannot really throw, but they are given pieces of candy and soft items to drop over the sides of the roof. The adults on the roof throw in all directions to the calls from below of "Over here! Throw over here!" and when a bucket of water is thrown over the roof everyone below shrieks and laughs and jumps aside.

No one below knows what will come over the roof next — something good to eat or water to soak the clothes and drench the hair.

On the roof "throwing"

BAKING BREAD FOR FEAST DAY
(Cochiti Pueblo)

The baking of bread in the outside horno is a major procedure, a job made easier when there are several women in the family and the weather is cooperative with the event.

For a feast day, fifty pounds of flour or more are often used; that amount of flour will make enough bread for one firing in a medium-sized oven.

At this house, the dough is mixed in the evening and left to rise overnight in a large galvanized tub. In the morning, the women shape the dough and place it in round greased pans. While the dough is rising again, one of the women, using kindling, starts a fire in the horno. Wood is added to the fire several times, until the oven becomes very hot.

When the oven seems hot enough, one of the women places a bucket of water near the horno and, with a heavy rag mop on a wooden pole, mops the ashes out of the oven. This action is repeated many times, and it is hot, heavy work.

The hot coals and ashes are then raked away from the horno. When the inside of the oven is cleaned out, a woman crumbles a piece of newspaper and tosses it to the center of the oven, or else sprinkles a little cornmeal in the oven's center; the temperature of the oven can be judged by watching the paper or cornmeal turn brown. If it burns or flames, the oven is too hot, and the oven must be mopped again.

When the oven has the correct temperature, all the family members are needed to carry the loaves of bread from the kitchen to the horno, while one woman, using a long wooden paddle, places the bread in the oven.

The heat is then controlled by covering the oven door halfway or all the way with a piece of wood. Fifty minutes to an hour is usually required for the bread to be nicely baked.

Next, the bread pans are removed with the paddle, and the freshly baked bread loaves are put on a clean cloth in the galvanized tub and carried into the house. Everyone gathers around to taste a loaf of bread, and there is nothing better than freshly baked hot bread from the horno.

Baking bread for Feast Day

THE PLACE THE SONGS COME FROM
(Cochiti Pueblo)

The men singers are standing at the edge of the plaza. Their voices rise and fall and at times are overpowered by the beat of the drum.

The singers range in age from the late seventies down to small boys who stand near their fathers or grandfathers.

The hand gestures of the singers are beautiful and signify the meaning of the songs: their forearms are raised and lowered; the hands make circles and are raised, palms upward, and lowered, palms downward, as they "speak" of clouds and rains and growing corn, and of hunters and animals, and of the warmth of the sun and the importance of the snow. They "speak" of the dependency of people on the mother earth and of all the things that nature provides. They "speak" of the interrelationship of all living things.

One of the older singers said, "Sometimes people, outsiders, think that what we do is silly, that our dances and songs aren't meaningful. But when we dance and when we sing, we are giving thanks for the good health of all people, not just Indian people, but all people. We are saying prayers for all the people of the world and for all living things. I give thanks for being able to make jewelry, and for my good health so I can make the jewelry, and for the earth that gives me all of my designs. When I was younger, I wrote many songs about how I felt about the hills and the mountains and the clouds. Now I don't write so many songs any more. But I always give thanks. That is what we do with our songs and our dances."

And now this man stands in the group of singers. Down the row from him is his daughter's father-in-law; close by is his son; in the plaza, dancing, are his daughters and grandchildren; in front of the house are many other relatives. As he sings and gives thanks, he is surrounded by many generations of people, to whom he is bonded by blood, marriage, or friendship. And the presence of the ancestors long departed are also felt in the plaza.

This is a wonderful thing; this is a special connection to the earth, to the very forces of life itself—the singing of songs of thankfulness, appreciation, and recognition, and the dancing in bare or moccasined feet upon the earth to the beat of the drum and the sounds of mens' voices. Indeed, these are experiences and rituals that sadly are long lost in the history of most cultural groups. This has substance; this has meaning; this connects the soul and thoughts of a person to all humanity, to the earth, to the sky, and to all of life.

The place the songs come from

KOSHARE WITH SNOW CONE
(Santa Domingo Pueblo)

The koshares—the clowns. Their dance gestures symbolize the meanings of the dance; they move with ease and grace and the gestures of their hands "help" the rain to fall and the corn to grow.

Wearing black loincloths, their bodies painted in black and white stripes, their hair tied up in two upright "pony tails" decorated with cornhusks, they dance.

The koshares dance an age-old dance with ancient symbolism. How beautifully they move. The koshares, their gestures, everyone watches them with feelings of awe and respect.

And here comes a koshare in this age-old dance—eating a snow cone.

Koshare with Snow Cone

WEDDING FEAST
(Santa Domingo Pueblo)

The wedding was held early in the morning on this September day, and now food is being served at the groom's family house, the bride's family house, and at their sponsor's house.

At the bride's family house, a large old adobe surrounded by shade trees at the edge of the village, there are many people sitting on the porch and standing in the dirt road, talking with friends and neighbors.

Children come and go from the house, finding it more fun to be outside and free to roam around the village.

It is cool inside the house with its thick adobe walls and high ceilings. The guests are sitting on chairs and benches along the walls and at the long dining table.

The bride, wearing a traditional black manta, and the groom in a contemporary suit, are standing at one end of the room, greeting their guests.

The older women, hair in bangs and wrapped in the back in a "chonga," wearing shawls, aprons, print dresses, stockings, and moccasins, are enjoying visiting together and watching the events of the day. The older men, bandannas tied around their foreheads, stand together near the door.

The long table is laden with food: bread pudding, fry bread, oven bread, tortillas, jello with marshmallows, and many kinds of salads, and turkey, ham, red and green chile, chile stews, posole, bowls of potato chips and bowls of candy, and cakes and cookies and fruit pies, and a large elaborate wedding cake. And to drink there is coffee, Kool Air, soda pop, and iced tea.

When people finish eating, they leave the table so others may sit down.

The festivities will continue all day, and people will go to the three houses to visit friends and eat, and to give good advice and blessings and prayers to the wedding couple.

Wedding Feast

ALL SOULS' DAY EVE
(San Felipe Pueblo)

Observance of All Souls' Day is a custom that has traveled over the centuries, via the Catholic church, from Europe to Mexico in the New World, and northward to most of the Pueblo Indian villages in New Mexico; the custom has blended with Pueblo customs and beliefs about death.

It is a good custom; it is the day the dead come back for a visit. Everyone has family or friends who are coming back, and their return is celebrated.

The smell of pinon wood fills the air on this fall night that is so crisp and cold with a full moon outlining the shapes of the corrals, sheds, and houses against the background of the dark mesa.

Groups of men are singing in the plaza, which is in the dark except for the moonlight, and sparks from a large fire in the churchyard rise in the air and can be seen against the dark sky.

Another group of men is in the churchyard, and the church bell rings out loud and clear in the cold night air.

At each house the women have prepared food, and friends and relatives visit each other's houses; later the women will take bundles of food to the church.

The church bells continue to ring throughout the night and the men continue singing; it is All Souls' Day Eve.

All Souls' Day Eve

NIGHT OF THE CORN DANCE
(Jemez Pueblo)

The dances are over, and it is very quiet in the village on this cool November evening.

There are many Navajos in the pueblo, because the histories of the Navajo and Jemez peoples have been entwined for many centuries.

They have gone through good and bad times together. At times they fought against each other, and at other times they helped each other at great risk to their own well-being.

Nowadays out of respect for each other and their long history together, and their many generations of friendships and inter-marriages, they attend each other's ceremonies.

In this old two-room adobe house, with its wood cook stove and chile ristras hanging from the vigas, the Pueblo women serve food and say to their Navajo and Pueblo visitors, "Come in, sit down, sit down and eat." Some of the Pueblo people speak a little of the Navajo language and say "gohweeh" as they pass the coffee across the table. "Ahehee" say the Navajos, "thank you."

A Pueblo man enters the kitchen bringing with him more Navajo friends, and there are smiles and the soft murmur of voices as people greet each other.

Night of the Corn Dance

WAITING FOR THE SHALAKO
(Zuni Pueblo)

It is always cold when the Shalako kachinas come for it is almost the time of the winter solstice.

It is after midnight, and each of the six Shalakos is at a house that has either had rooms added to it or has been totally built for a Shalako.

The walls of the rooms where the Shalakos will dance are covered with colorful blankets. Above the blankets hang shawls, folded blankets, fringed blankets, concho belts, beads, and scarves. The room is a kaleidoscope of colors and patterns.

The inside of each house is filled with people patiently waiting for the Shalako to dance. Outside the houses, people are standing quietly, looking in the windows, because there isn't room for everyone in the houses.

The earth feels hard and cold beneath booted feet, and breath can be seen in the air. People speak in hushed voices because to see the Shalako kachina, to witness and participate by watching, is a great privilege.

As with most Pueblo ceremonies, prayers are said for all the people of the world, for the earth and what the earth provides, for rain, for the relationship of man and plants and animals and the rain. This is a night of prayer. The people say thank you with prayer songs and dance, and these prayer songs last for many hours.

Anticipation fills the air. About to appear is a wondrous being, older than anyone can say, a spectacular combination of man, animal, bird, imagination, and metaphysical forces, put to visual imagery in mask and dance and pageantry.

Looking in the windows waiting for the Shalako

THE SHALAKO APPEARS
(Zuni Pueblo)

The Shalako mask rests on the floor, standing tall, over a man's height. Behind it are the two Shalako impersonators; slumped in their chairs, with white-capped heads nodding towards their chests, blankets wrapped around their bodies for warmth, they sleep.

The singers, men of all ages wearing headbands of folded scarves, are in another corner, talking quietly and smoking. Soon they will start to sing, holding rattles in their right hands; their voices and the shake of the rattles will be continuous for many hours.

Against another wall a row of men are sitting on a bench, some sleeping, some awake and waiting in silence.

An elderly blanketed man wakes up, stands, and moves to the Shalako mask, and two other blanketed men join him. They open their arms and their blankets fan out forming a screen. Now the Shalako mask can't be seen except for a few feathers showing above their blankets. For what seems a long time, the men stand there with their arms held at shoulder level and their blankets making brilliant patterns and colorful stripes. And then, in a split second, it happens! The Shalako rises! The blanketed men step back, and there it is--the Shalako! He begins to dance. Until dawn, the dance and song will continue.

His long beak "clacks" as he patters across the room. His feathers shine; his long hair gleams. He sways, dips, runs, and the beak "clack clacks." Oh, he is a spectacular, breathtaking being!

Little children watch him, wide-eyes but without fear. A baby waves her tiny arms in time to the beat of the rattles, and the Shalako leans toward the baby, and "clack" goes his beak. The spectators chuckle. The baby smiles. Someone peels an orange, and its aroma fills the room. The hosts pass out soft drinks, and people gladly accept them.

People are tired as the night wears on. It is very cold outside but hot and stuffy inside the house. Legs ache from standing, and everyone feels the need for sleep. But the Shalako dances, and the magic and mystery of the Shalako keeps everyone there.

The Shalako appears

WATCHING WINTER DANCES
(Cochiti Pueblo)

There have been dances on Christmas day and each of the four days after Christmas. On this day, the fourth day, there is an eagle dance; the eagle dancers, escorted by an elderly man, enter the plaza.

The eagle dancers cast wonderful shadows on the ground as their bodies lean forward at the waist and their arms, outstretched like wings and covered with feathers, tilt and swoop gracefully.

Worldwide the eagle has been endowed with symbolism, for the eagle is strong, proud, fierce, and free; the eagle is a messenger between earth and sky, between man and the gods.

Standing on one side of the plaza are the singers wrapped in blankets; their backs make a blaze of colors and patterns.

An elderly woman stands outside a house, watching the dances and holding a bundle. Someone takes her a chair and a cup of hot tea, and she gratefully sits down, puts the bundle on the ground beside her, and hugs the cup with her hands.

A dog saunters over, sits next to the woman, and appears to watch the dances also.

Later the woman unwraps the cotton cloth covering a basket filled with fruit and soft drinks. Walking slowly, she takes the basket to the group in the plaza. After presenting the basket, she reaches into an apron pocket for a pinch of cornmeal. She sprinkles the sacred cornmeal on the ground and returns to her chair.

Women with dog, bundle and hot tea watching the winter dances

GETTING READY FOR THE PARADE
(Navajo Fair at Window Rock)

The sky is a sheet of gray, the cold September rain is pouring down, people are trying to organize the decorated floats, and the traffic in Window Rock is backed up for many miles. But it is a calm traffic jam, and everyone is very pleasant because there is nothing that can be done about either the traffic or the rain; eventually both will pass.

The drivers of the trucks and cars finally find parking places past the fairgrounds on the road to Ganado, and people stand in the back of their trucks and on top of cars trying to see if the parade is getting started.

The normally quiet street is filled with people wrapped in shawls and blankets of every color and pattern, wearing hats and holding umbrellas and pieces of plastic and newspapers over their heads.

At last the parade starts down the road, and all get out of their vehicles and stand along the roadside. It is still raining and a few people try to balance umbrellas as they focus their cameras.

Here they come: the Marines on horseback, the Navajo Code Talkers who were in World War II, marching bands, a group of elderly men on horseback with backs so straight and their faces lined and handsome. Navajo girls and women looking very chilled and wearing the beautiful traditional clothing, floats with Navajo rock bands, and the governors of the states of New Mexico and Arizona.

Eventually the parade is over and everyone starts down the road toward the "rainbow," the big rainbow arch symbolic of the way of life of "the people": the marks the entrance to the fairgrounds.

Getting ready for the parade

IN THE LIVESTOCK BUILDING
(Navajo Fair at Window Rock)

All morning the earth has been drenched with a cold, chilling rain, and the fairgrounds are deep in mud, and shoes make squishy sounds at each step.

In spite of the weather there are people at the horse races, the rodeo, food booths, craft booths, produce and livestock buildings, and almost every other event at the fair.

The livestock building is crowded with animals and people, and the powwow is being held at one end of the building because it is much too wet to have a powwow outside.

People are walking slowly about, taking their time looking at sheep. Serious-sounding conversations are going on as people pause, look, and discuss, and walk on to look at the next row of sheep.

Raising sheep has been one of the mainstays of Navajo life for many centuries. Sheep are used for food, the wool is sold, and the wool is also used for the exquisite weavings made by Navajo people.

The sheep are all beautifully groomed and seem to take it for granted that they should be the object of so much attention.

In the livestock building

FRY BREAD CONTEST
(Navajo Nation Fair at Window Rock)

The fry bread contest is under way and a crowd is gathering; people are filling the bleachers, and other people stop as they pass the open side of the building, and stand and watch.

Inside the large building the women are busy making fry bread. The women wear velvet blouses, long full print skirts, and aprons, and have their hair tied up and covered with scarves.

Each woman has her own pan over an open fire, her own ingredients, and work area. The women, carrying the long-handled forks, walk back and forth from the work area to the open fires. Bending over the fire is hot work; the fry bread dough is put into the hot oil, and a few minutes later it comes out golden brown and smelling delicious.

A judge of the contest once said that as much as she loved to eat fry bread, after the first ten pieces it became a very difficult contest to judge.

Fry bread contest

NAVAJO POTTERY NAVAJO NATION FAIR
(Navajo Nation Fair at Window Rock)

This is not the polished black pottery, exquisite in its simplicity, of San Ildefonso and Santa Clara pueblos; nor is it covered with intricate painted designs, like the pottery of Acoma or Zia. This pottery looks utilitarian, durable; it has a humble elegance. It is pottery that came from need and use—everyday use and ceremonial use—and aesthetics were of second importance.

Navajo pottery was meant to be held; it could be called "a people's pottery."

Nowadays some of the pottery has obtained status as art. Some is made in the shapes of animals; some is made for ceremonial use and some for utilitarian use. There is a wide variety of styles and techniques being used today, but all this pottery has a feeling of warmth. The mottled browns, the curves that fit so well into the hands, the shine of the pinon-pitch coating—this is pottery of the earth for the people.

In the long process of getting the clay from the earth, making the pot, firing the pot, and pitching the pot, the making of pottery follows old and important traditions and often involves more members of the family than just the person making the pottery.

At the Window Rock fair, the pottery of Faye Tso, a famous potter and herbalist, and the pottery of her daughters, can be found, and sometimes the pottery of Penny Emerson and Jimmy Wilson.

There are always people gathered around Faye Tso's booth. Some are buying pots for ceremonial use; others are buying herbs and clay pipes; several people are buying more decorative pieces.

Navajo pottery

EATING MUTTON STEW
(Navajo Fair at Window Rock)

By midnight it is getting very cold, and people hunch down in their jackets and wrap blankets and shawls around themselves, as gusts of wind whip down the midway scattering scraps of paper and blowing sand.

The lights of the carnival are beginning to dim, the bleachers are starting to empty of people at the powwow, the rodeo is over, and the rock concert is ending.

The midway becomes crowded with people once again, and now everyone is looking for food booths.

People hug their coffee cups for warmth while they order fry bread and mutton stew.

Everyone looks very tired; it is midnight at the fair.

Eating mutton stew

FALL DAY IN CANYON DE CHELLY

The canyon is not only beautiful; it has an aura of history, of mystery, of secrecy.

On the north walls of the canyon, high above the canyon floor, are cliff houses built by the Anasazi. The voices of those ancient ones, echoing down the canyon, can almost be heard today.

The canyon was lived in continuously for a thousand years by the Anasazi, the ancestors of today's Pueblo people, by the Hopi, who tended fruit orchards, and later by the Navajo.

Today, in this quiet place of great beauty, the Navajo people tend sheep and raise corn. In the fall, gentle breezes flicker the leaves of the cottonwood trees, and after a rain, a warm stream of water flows along the canyon floor.

Women in full skirts and velveteen blouses, their fingers and wrists covered with rings and bracelets, walk along with their sheep. Here and there a man on horseback appears; outside a hogan, a woman works at her loom. Life is pleasant.

For children, the canyon is a marvelous playground: streams to wade in, rock formations to climb, the mysteries of the cliff houses and wonders of the pictographs and petroglyphs. And, of course, there is the job of sheep herding.

The sound of the engine of a "6x" vehicle can be heard as it carries a group of tourists touring down the canyon. But the tourists are quiet; the canyon evokes feelings of awe in everyone, for here, one realizes that nature is so much more powerful and enduring than man.

Later in the fall, when the canyon starts to trap the cold weather between its walls, people will take the sheep, horses, and other livestock out of the canyon, and all will go to live above, in and around the town of Chinle.

A fall day in Canyon De Chelly

POWWOW
(Tsaile)

The powwow (social and competitive dances) takes place in the gymnasium of the Navajo Community College at Tsaile. Craft and food booths are placed along the walls, and many people circulate around the room talking with friends, looking at the crafts, and sampling fry bread and Navajo tacos. During the Grand Entry there is an overwhelming array of beautiful dance costumes; fancy dancers, fancy shawl dancers, war dancers, straight dancers, women's northern and southern buckskin dancers, and on and on come the dancers until they have filled the whole dance area.

There are children in dance costumes, and young adults, middle-aged people, and a few very old people. There are beaded moccasins, feathers, and leather leggings and dresses. There are splashes of color and the sounds of bells and the pad of moccasins on the floor; there are flashes of braids and shawls as a fancy shawl dancer whirls past. A dog dancer crouches and quivers, his head darts from side to side, and his movements are swift. A straight dancer glides by, and the fancy dancers twirl and whirl leaving the eye to see only a blaze of color.

Sitting in the bleachers are people of all ages. There are old women wearing many full skirts and velvet blouses, their hair covered with scarves, men in western dress, girls with permed hair wearing jeans, college students, and mothers and babies. And always there is the flash of silver—a heavy concho belt at the waist of a velvet blouse, a ketoh on a brown wrist, and a hand smoothing back hair is heavy with silver and turquoise rings.

The sounds of singing and rums will fill the air for hours to come.

Powwow at Tsaile

GLOSSARY

Adobe   Mud brick.

Ahehee   Thank you (Navajo).

Anasazi   Navajo word meaning "the ancient ones," the first in-habitants of Canyon de Chelly. The Anasazi entered the Southwest about the first century to A.D. 1300. They were changing from hunters and gatherers to farmers and eventually built the stone cliff houses in the canyon.

Banner   A long pole used during the Corn dance from which hangs a dance kilt, eagle feathers, and fox pelt, topped with parrot feathers; sun symbol; waved over the dancers as a blessing to the dancers and the pueblo. Possibly of Aztec origin.

Canyon de Chelly   Pronounced "shay." The pronunciation of the Navajo word *Tsegi*, meaning "rock canyon," was changed by the Spanish, until it came to be pronounced "shay." Located near the town of Chinle on the Navajo Reservation, Canyon de Chelly consists of three steep canyons that are 500 to 700 feet deep.

Gohweeh   Coffee (Navajo).

Horno   Outside oven made of adobe; design brought to the Americas by the Spaniards.

Kachina   Can be the mask or doll (carving) that represents the spirit; can be the man who dons the mask and becomes the spirit; can be the force of energy of the spirit.

Keresan   The language spoken at some of the pueblos (Acoma, Zia, Cochiti, San Felipe, Santo Domingo, Laguna, Santa Ana).

Ketoh   Wrist guard (Navajo).

Kiva   Ceremonial building, circular in shape; the shape of the building and objects in the kiva are symbolic of man's beginning and place in the universe.

Koshare   The koshares play many roles. They are clown figures; they are in charge of the spectators and dancers; they help the dancers with repairs to their dance clothing;

	and they have the power to bring on the rain and help the corn to grow.
Manta	Traditional black wool dress tied at the waist, usually open over the left shoulder; worn for tablita dances and various ceremonial functions.
Navajo code Talkers	During World War II, Navajo men served as a platoon in the Signal Corps in the Pacific. The Navajo language was used as a code across enemy lines. They became known as the "code talkers."
The People	The Navajo word dine means "the people."
Petroglyphs	Symbols or pictures incised on rocks and canyon walls.
Pictographs	Paintings on rocks and canyon walls by the Anasazi (and in Canyon de Chelly by the Navajo and Hopi as well).
Posole	Hominy stew.
Powwow	Social and competitive dances; most of the dances are of Plains origin.
Ristra	Ristra of chile, string of chile, usually dried in the sun in the fall, then hung in the kitchen to be used in cooking.
Shalako	Kachinas that embody all aspects of the life cycles and bring blessing and prayers for all people. The Shalako mask is one of the largest in the world.
Tablita	Women's headdress made of thin wooden boards, with cut-out patterns of cloud, sun and star symbols. Worn during the Corn Dance (tablita dance).
Vigas	Round wooden beams, roof supports.
Zuni Pueblo	Located 40 miles south of Gallup. It was the first pueblo entered by the Spanish conquistadors. The language of Zuni is spoken only at Zuni.

ORIGIN OF THROW DAYS

The exact origin of throw days seems to be uncertain, but it is said that they date back to pre-Spanish times and that they were held at the time of the harvest.

Before there was money to exchange, the Pueblos were completely communal: land, food, shelter, and the welfare of the village people were all communal matters.

According to oral history, the produce from the fields was taken to the kivas where many of the village people fasted for four days. The food was then given to the people who had fasted and was afterward distributed to the rest of the people of the village.

It is possible that this Pueblo custom blended with a pre-Christian European custom that was incorporated in the Catholic church of throwing in celebration, the harvest, the fruits of the earth.

Because of the Spanish rule over the Pueblo people for more than a hundred years until the Pueblo Revolt in 1680, many of the Pueblo customs were maintained and preserved only by blending them with holy days and religious holidays of the Catholic Church.

Today, throw days are held on saints' days. Usually if a family member is named after a saint, the family will throw on that particular saint's day.

Today a throw day is a costly event as almost all of the objects are purchased and the throwers are more than generous in the quantity of their throw items—as in the early days, the Pueblo people share.